The Mini Bo

By Dave Dutton

Introduction

They say there are only three ways of dealing with an insult. . .
The first is to ignore it.
The second is to give the person delivering it a thump on the nose.
The third is to top it with a better one. . .
I suspect that most of us ordinary mortals would find the first course
of action extremely difficult, the second inadvisable and the third
well-nigh ruddy impossible. . . Most of us faced with such a situation
would probably slink away only to agonize in the middle of the night
as to the crushing rejoinder we would have uttered - if only we could
have thought of one at the time.The French call it esprit de l'escalier
- staircase wit - or the witty remark that occurs to one after the
opportunity to make it has been lost.
How often have we envied the capabilities of the top cabaret
comedians who, when confronted by some intrusive heckler, have
effortlessly and swiftly reduced that selfsame heckler to a quivering
laughing-stock by instantly responding with merciless quick-fire
one-liners. . .?
What most people don't realize is that those comedians have a ready
stock of 'heckler-stoppers' on which to draw in any emergency. What
sounds like an ad-lib is in fact a carefully-laid trap for the unwary.
The right retort for the right occasion. . .
Which is what this mini ebook is all about... in attempting to provide
the right retort for the right occasion I have compiled hundreds of
put-downs, squelches, insults and quips guaranteed to give that extra
edge in any verbal joust.
As Hazlitt said: 'He who puts up with insult invites injury'. So don't. .
.
Do what the professionals do - memorise some of the insults to use
as and when the occasion demands and you'll soon gain a reputation
for having a razor-sharp wit far in excess of your actual capabilities.
It will be totally undeserved of course. But then, only you and I will
know that... won't we?
PS: We take no responsibility for any use of these insults and
putdowns. You use them at your own risk! After all - they're *your*
teeth...

TOP OF THE UNPOPS

Or how to let people know they score ZILCH on a popularity rating of 1-10 . . .

You grow on people - like superfluous hair.

You're as welcome as piles on a pushbike.

You're as welcome as a hang-glider with diarrhoea.

You're like a side of bacon - you'd improve with hanging.

I hope that a dog on heat falls in love with your shin.

You're as welcome as a crack in a glass eye.

She's as popular as rabies in a guide dogs' home.

They're as welcome as a dog with a wet nose in a nudist colony.

I see that you always dress to kill. Your breath has the same effect on people too.

You're as welcome as a pork chop in a synagogue.

You're as welcome as a French kiss at a family reunion. .

He's so unpopular you have to queue up to hate him.

He's taking lessons in deportment. Three more, then they deport him.

His workmates call him 'Vick' because he gets up people's noses.

He spreads joy and happiness whenever he goes.

I bet that with a little practice, you could be really unpleasant.. .

Why don't you kiss me under the mistletoe? It's tied to the end of my shirt lap.

You'd look lovely in blue. Go and jump in the sea.

I'd like to shake you warmly by the throat.

Excuse me but you'd make a very good stranger.

I like the way you throw yourself into your work - I only wish you worked on a sewage farm.

I wouldn't say she was unpopular, but she had little marks all over her where men had touched her with 10-foot bargepoles.

Talk to you? I'd sooner have all my teeth pulled out without gas.

You have all the charm of an unflushed loo.

People like you don't grow on trees - they swing from them.

I wish that I was a pigeon and you were a statue.

There are no flies on you - well, even flies can be particular.

Did you get that face through eating too many sour grapes?

He lights up a room - when he leaves it.

He's very musical - even his feet hum

Next time you're passing our house, I'd be grateful.

He was an unwanted baby - his parents had him baptized in boiling water. They bought him a rattle - with a snake on the other end.

His mother used to send him out to steal hubcaps off moving cars.

I wouldn't say that his parents didn't like him but his mother used to wrap his school packed lunch in a road map.

He was so unpopular at school that when he played Hide and Seek, nobody went to look for him.

When they played Doctors and Nurses at school, they made him the ambulance driver.

When I say he was teacher's pet. I mean she used to keep him in a cage at the back of the class.

He's as popular with people as Colonel Sanders is with chickens.

He's as popular as woodworm in a crutch.

He said 'Why do people take an instant dislike to me?' I told him: 'Because it saves time.'

I wouldn't say he was unpopular, but when he phoned the Samaritans, they told him to sod off.

He does great work for all the hospitals in his neighbourhood - he makes people sick.

I wish you were a lamp-post and I were a dog.

He's invited to all the best houses in town - once.

You'd look nice in something flowing madam. Why don't you jump in the river?

Why don't you bore a hole in your head and let all the sap run out?

You look like a bowel movement waiting to happen.

Why don't you go and play on the motorway?

They wanted to have him on This is Your Life, but they couldn't find anybody who would admit to being his friend.

There's a bus leaving in ten minutes - be under it.

Why don't you take a long walk on a short pier?

Get back to the sewage farm - they're missing a bag of shit.

How would I like to speak to you? Through a medium.

Why don't you ask your owner to take you for a walk?

I have a soft spot for you - it's called quicksand.

When he was born, his father threw bricks at the stork.

He's known as 'Flatulence' because when you get rid of him, it's a great relief.

Why don't you broaden your mind? - stick your head under a steamroller.

He was invited to a small bore shooting club. Then they stood him on a box and took potshots at him.

He's too lazy to mow the back garden - in fact the grass is so long his wife has to peg the clothes out on horseback. .

If all of his friends got together, there wouldn't be enough people for a game of draughts.

If you can take to her, you can plait jam.

He's a transvestite gourmet - in other words, he wants to eat, drink and be Mary.

Remind me to call your parents if I want the blueprint to make an arsehole.

His breath smells so much that he has to chew Odor Eaters.

No one wants to go with her because she has dandruff so bad that her crabs wear snowshoes.

If he ever wanted a friend, he'd have to buy a dog.

You're as popular as a fart in a spacesuit.

The first woman he ever made love to was a suffragette - and then only because she was chained to some railings at the time.

I wouldn't say he was an alcoholic, but at his post-mortem, his liver won a breakdancing competition.

He's about as popular as cold lavatory seats.

Potted putdowns pertaining to people's personal proclivities...

If you and your brother put your heads together, you'd have enough wood to make a shed.

You're like Horlicks - you send me to sleep.

He has breath like an armpit with teeth

I knew you when you were alive

She's a girl of but eighteen Summers - and forty-two Winters.

If they can make penicillin out of a bit of mouldy bread, surely they can make something out of you.

You're like an ancient Greek instrument - an old lyre.

Try the Lost Property Office - they might have your brain.

He researched his family tree - and found out that half of them were still living in it.

He's very level-headed - in fact the drink dribbles out evenly from both comers of his mouth.

If your wit were shit, you'd be constipated.

He's a good advert for abortions.

He can tell lies and prove them.

He has a well-balanced personality - a chip on both shoulders.

Lazy? He once spent five weeks off work with a broken flask.

Talk about lazy? There's more life in a tramp's vest

When he drops something on the floor, he waits until his shoelaces need tying before he picks it up

His version of the 23rd psalm begins: 'The Dole is my Shepherd, I shall not work ..'

He's so idle, he thinks a P45 is a revolver.

He's superstitious - he won't go to work on any day with a 'y'-in it.

He wouldn't pee on you if you were on fire.

The only active thing about him is when his nose runs.

He joined a dozen trade unions so that he would always be on strike.

His feet are filthy - he hasn't been to the seaside this year.

He's a shift worker - as soon as you mention work, he shifts. ,

His workmates call him The Blister - because he only shows up after the work is done.

When he wants to take a bubble bath, he has beans the night before.

When he wants to take a shower, he pees into a fan.

She's the original good time that was had by all.

She's seen more prick ends than a dartboard.

She can trip you up and be under you before you hit the ground.

The safest place to bide money in their house is under the soap.

The Dead Sea was alive - until he paddled his feet in it.

You're as much use as a chocolate teapot.

He's lower than whaleshit - and that's at the bottom of the ocean.

The boys call her Angel Delight - because she's easy to make.

They call her 'Blackpool' because everybody's been there.

She'll go with you for peanuts - then come back for the shells.

She's known to her boyfriends as 'Yo Yo Knickers'.

She's been picked up so many times, she's got handles on her hips.

She's been in the back ot so many parked cars that the AA show her on their route maps. .

They call her 'Quaker' because you can get her down without a fight.

I wouldn't say that she's oversexed, but she's got callouses on her shoulder-blades.

When she dies, they'll have to bury her in a Y-shaped coffin..

She's had more men than the Grand Old Duke of York.

She comes from a posh family - she puts newspaper under the cuckoo clock and has ashtrays with no adverts on them.

He smokes so many cigarettes that if you painted a white line down the middle of his tongue, it would look like a tarmacadam road.

She's been with so many sailors, her hips go in and out with the tide.

They're so stuck up that when their lavatory's engaged, they announce it in The Times.

When I look at you, I realize that all the nuts aren't in Brazil.

She's known locally as The Bedspread because she's been turned down so often.

She's a very humble person - but then again she has a lot to be humble about,

He's the kind of bloke who'd steal the corn from under a blind chicken's nose.

He's so mean that he's glad he was born illegitimate because it saves him having to buy any cards for Father's Day.

Don't try to insult me -I've been insulted by experts!

When she gets up in the morning, she has two washes - one for each face.

If he's sane then I don't want to be.

He's enough grease on his hair to make a pan of chips.

He's a joiner. If he sees anyone going into a pub, he joins them.

Talk about a boozer - he's had his toes amputated so he can stand nearer to the bar.

When they gave out brains he thought they said 'drains' so he picked a sewer instead.

His neck is covered in love bites - most of them self-inflicted.

If you're so clever, how come you aren't rich?

Why don't you save on fuel bills? Drop dead.

You have a very bright future behind you.

He has two stomachs for food - and none for work.

He's mentioned in the Bible - where it says 'And. the Lord made all manner of creeping things . . .'

In any rose garden, you always get a few little pricks. .

Go and lean against the wall -: that's plastered. too.

You're a very humble person. Mind you, you've a lot to be humble about.

You're as much use as a glass hammer.

She's as pure as the driven slush.

The difference between him and a coconut is that can get a drink out of a coconut.

In case you're wondering what your IQ is, don't worry - it's nothing.

He's not really gay - he only helps them out when they're busy.

His mates call him Pea Soup, because he's thick, green and wet..

He wanted to be a human being - but he failed the medical.

You've got an ear for music - Van Gogh's.

There are no flies on you - your breath sees to that.

I'll speak to you later- through an interpreter.

I wouldn't say he's a crawler - he's just addicted to boot polish..

I'll say this about him. He changes his socks regularly - from one foot to the other.

She's such a snob that she has monogrammed bags under her eyes.

He only drinks on two occasions - when it's raining and when it's not.

He's such a snob that he refuses to travel in the same car as his chauffeur.

If brains were a disease, you'd be healthy.

He's a constipated alcoholic - he can't pass a pub.

When his wife told him she wanted a foreign car for her birthday, he bought her a rickshaw.

His wristwatch is so old that Mickey Mouse has arthritis in both legs.

He got in trouble at the zoo for feeding the monkeys - to the lions.

Of course prostitutes have babies - where do you think traffic wardens come from?

When he applied to join the Open University, they shut it.

When he sings 'Danny Boy' people cry -... especially music lovers.

He's so nasty, he sellotapes worms to the lawn and watches the sparrows get ruptures.

What makes you laugh - open graves?

He's an all-time loser. . . always sucking his own trumpet.

He's picked his nose so much that he's pulled the lining out of his cap.

His mother always said he would come out on top. He did - he went bald.

You remind me of a kipper - spineless, yellow and two-faced.

They're like a bunch of bananas - there's not a straight one amongst them.

They've got more twists than a game of pontoon.

He's very good to his mother - he never goes home.

How would you like your teeth for your supper?

He's the kind of man you shake hands with – and then count your fingers.

He's so common that when he's playing at cards and he picks up a Spade, he spits on his hands.

His grandfather was a peer - and his grandmother had kidney trouble too.

She never sleeps with anyone unless he's a friend - and she hasn't an enemy in the world.

He's a member of the Dipsomatic Corps. ..:.

He's as much use as a balloon without skin.

I wouldn't say he drinks a lot, but when the police took a blood sample off him, it had a head on it.

He has a company that exports bull - in fact he's the biggest bullshipper in town.

I'm not saying she sleeps around, but she's been in more beds than Alan Titchmarsh.

What a moneygrabber. He'd work through the two minutes' silence if you paid him time-and-a-half.

He's so devious, he could go in a revolving door behind you - and come out in front of you.

Her family came over with William the Conqueror. Mind you, the immigration laws are much stricter now.

He once found a crutch - so he went home and broke his wife's leg.

He can light a cigarette in his trouser pocket.

He was so dirty as a kid that the teacher used him as the blackboard.

He goes to a fancy dress as Napoleon - so he can keep his hand on his wallet.

He has so many empty beer bottles in his back yard, it's put £2000 on the value of the house.

When he gets up in the morning, he looks under the bed to see if he's lost any sleep.

He wouldn't give you the steam off his pee.

He wouldn't give a lavatory door a bang.

I wouldn't say he was mean but he's like a Scotsman with all the generosity wrung out of
 him.

He's so mean he told his little boy that the gas meter was a piggy bank.

He's as tight as a duck's arse - and that's watertight.

He's too mean to buy laxatives for his kids - he sits them on the potty and tells them ghost stories.

He's so mean, he switches the gas off when he turns the bacon over in the frying-pan.

To save buying his little boy a pair of shoes, he repainted his feet black and laced his toes together.

He's so mean that he uses *both* sides of the toilet paper.

If he'd a faceful of pimples he wouldn't give you one.

He goes to the park to pinch bread off the ducks.

He'll never get piles - God made him the perfect arsehole.

There's a lot less to you than meets the eye.

He's as subtle as an air-raid.

She's such a prude that she rides her pushbike cross-legged.

I admire the way you love nature - in spite of what it's done to you.

She's so frigid that when she opens her legs, a little light pops on.

He's such a gentleman. He gets out of the bath to have a pee in the sink. .

I hope that next time you jump on a bicycle, it hasn't got a seat.

He claims he's a self-made man. It's nice of him to take the blame.

He's as useless as a suck at blow football.

He has done for good manners what President Truman did for Hiroshima .

May you go to Heaven – and soon.

She has a mattress strapped to her back in case she comes across someone she knows.

I wouldn't say they had a dirty house, but you wipe your feet coming out.

He does more flapping than a tap-dancer's fanny.

He always sends his mother a 'congratulations' telegram on his birthday.

Did you leave your broomstick on a double yellow line?

I wouldn't say he plays with himself a lot, but his self-winding wristwatch is wound up until December 2026.

He's a Test Tube Baby - his father was a wanker.

She's so mean, she darns Kleenex.

I always call him Sir - spelt C-U-R.

The people in the office call him Tarzan - because he's always yelling and he likes to be surrounded by creepers.

He's nothing but a sadist - he goes round telling hypochondriacs how well they look.

She's known to the boys as the Pile of Pennies -because she's a pushover.

She's got a mind like concrete - all mixed up and permanently set.

He had two half-brothers and a half-sister - then his mother took the chain-saw off him.

He's such a miserable sod that the landlord throws him out of the pub when it's the Happy Hour.

He's a sincere hypocrite.

LOOKS AREN'T EVERYTHING

(Or, in your case, they're nothing - physiognomic insults of the not-very-nice kind. Please use them sparingly if you value your teeth...)

He's so ugly that when he looked out of a car window, the police arrested him for mooning.

Her nose is so big, her nostrils have an echo.

He's so thin that when he takes a shower, he has to run round to get wet.

His willy is so small that he once accidentally pulled out a hair and peed inside his trousers.

She's got black hair all down her back. None on her head - just her back.

Do you like his suit? Somewhere there's a car driving round without seat covers.

She's so fat that she has to use a boomerang to put a scarf on.

She's so thin that she needs a pair of braces to hold up her knickers.

You were born the wrong way up - your nose runs and your feet smell.

The only fur coat that she's likely to get is the one on her tongue.

Her face is so thin that she models for pirate's flags.

She's so ugly, she couldn't turn a bathtap on.

I'm not saying he had a tiny head, but he could look with both eyes through a monocle.

Her glasses are so big that when you stand in front of her, it's like window-shopping.

He has a nose like a one-eyed cobbler's thumb.

He was so ugly as a child that his mother had to tie a piece of raw meat around his neck so that the dog would play with him.

She's so ugly that you have to be over 18 to look at her.

When she opens the fridge door, the fish fingers go for her throat.

He was so ugly as a baby that the police made his mother fit Venetian blinds on the pram.
Even his poor old mother couldn't stand looking at him - she used to feed him with a catapult.

I've seen better heads on a pint of beer.

If Moses had seen her face, there would have been another Commandment.

Actually, her teeth are like the Ten Commandments - all broken.

If beauty's only skin deep, who peeled you?

What are you going to do for a face when King Kong wants his arse back?

How much do you charge for haunting houses?

She's a face that looks like it wore out two bodies.

You've got Scandinavian looks - or should I say you've a face like a Norse.

That Grecian 2000 you've been using has worked. Now you look like a 2000-year-old Greek.

When they had you circumcised, they threw the wrong bit away.

I like your hair. Did you spend your holidays in a wind tunnel - or did you come here on a motorbike?

I'm not saying he is bald, but from a distance, it looks like his neck's blowing bubble gum.

You can't tell whether he's bald or whether he's wearing a pink crash helmet.

He's not bald - he's wearing a flesh-coloured toupee.

Excuse me, would you mind covering your bald head up? The light's bouncing off and dazzling my eyes.

I'm not saying he's bald, but he's the only bloke l know who combs his hair with a duster.

He's not bald; he just has a very wide parting.

He's not bald - he just wears a see-through wig.

He had wavy hair and it waved him goodbye.

Is that a moustache - or has your eyebrow come down for a drink?

The last time I saw anything like that on a top lip, the whole herd had to be destroyed.

HE must be important - he's underlined his nose.

Is that a moustache or are you chewing a rat?

Are those patent leather shoes - or are you just incontinent
?
He looks like a badly-bungled embalming job.

You're not the ugliest woman I've ever seen – but you don't half look like her.

You can stop taking those Ugly Pills - you've had enough. I wouldn't say she had a big nose, but if she broke it, she'd have to have it put in a sling.

He had a face that only a mother could love.

From the side, her nose looks like a windsock in a stiff breeze.

She's so fat, she can answer the front door without leaving the kitchen.

I've seen tripe better dressed.

You've a face like the back of a tram-smash.

I wouldn't say she was a dwarf but the rain reaches her three seconds after everybody else.

You look like a rummage sale on legs.

They moved her away from the monkey-house at the zoo because her face was frightening the gorillas.

She's so ugly that parents keep her picture on the mantelpiece to keep the kids away from the fire.

She's a face like mouldy spam.

If you were a house, you'd be condemned.

He's got BO - but nobody's been near enough to tell him.

Who pinched the bolts from out of your neck?

I wouldn't say she's anorexic but when she goes put in a stiff breeze, she twangs.

She's so ugly that when she sucks a lemon, the lemon pulls a face.

She's so overweight, she can arrive in a crowd all by herself.

She's got a face like a dog's bum with a hat on it.

She got thrown out of alcoholics anonymous because when the others saw her, they thought they were having DTs.

You've a face like a bad ham.

She's so thin that she can't go to the pictures because she can't keep the seat down.

You should join the Ku Klux Klan - you'd look better with a bag over your head.

His name is Thursday because when his father saw him for the first time, he said: 'I think we'll call it a day.'

When the Mountains of Mourne swept down to the sea, they must have passed over her face.

She has a double chin - but her bottom lip hides it.

When they gave out noses, he thought they said roses - so he chose a great big red one.
 It must be a face - it's got ears on it!

She's so ugly, she gets fan mail from warthogs
.
He sent his photograph to a Lonely Hearts Club, and they sent it back saying: 'We're not that lonely!'

His nose is so big that when he and his twin brother stand back to back, they look like a pick.

With a face like yours, the only time you could pass for normal is on Hallowe'en.

Are those your own teeth '- or are you breaking them in for a horse?

The last time I saw a nose like yours, someone was feeding it buns.

I didn't believe Darwin's Theory of Evolution -until I laid eyes on you.

When she went to see a horror film, the audience thought it was Dracula making a personal appearance.

She's so gruesome that when she walks into a room, the mice throw themselves onto traps.
His face is a good cure for constipation.

When you get home tonight miss, throw your mother a bone from me.

She's so small that when she gets a suntan, she looks like a wholewheat loaf on legs.

Are you wearing that suit for a bet?

When she wants to make yogurt, she stares at a bottle of milk.

She's a sight that gives you sore eyes.

She's the sort of girl you dream about (when you've had cheese for your supper).

He eats like a pig - unfortunately the resemblance doesn't end there.

He has so many spots on his face; he looks like an advert in braille.

When she was a kid, her mother used to wet her lips and stick her on the window while she did the homework.

I wouldn't say he had acne but he looks like a pomegranate turned inside out.

He looks like an Eccles Cake with the top off.

He has eyes like bulldog's balls.

She's so ugly that once when she went missing, her husband gave her description to the
police -and they wouldn't believe him.

She's so fat that when her husband carried her across the threshold, he had to make three trips with a wheelbarrow.

He has striking teeth. One fell out - and the others all came out in sympathy.

He only has one tooth - in fact he can chew Polo Mints without breaking them.

She's so fat that her husband has to stand up in bed to see whether or not it's daylight.

You've got a face like an unmade bed.

She used to be a decoy for a whaling fleet.

Who cut your hair - the council?

She has more chins than a Chinese telephone directory.
Have you cut your hair with a knife and fork?

I'm not saying his lips are thick but when he whistles, he can't see where he's going.

You've got a face like a melted wellington.

She's got lips like a burst Walls pork sausage.

You've got a face like a ruptured custard.

That's lovely long blonde hair you have. It's a pity it's on your chin.

You've got a strange growth at the top of your' neck - it's your head.

The bags under her eyes are so big that it looks like her nose is wearing a saddle.

He's so small, he used to work as a lumberjack on a mushroom farm.

I'm not saying that you're tiny but my wife would like you for her charm bracelet.
You've got a face like a farmer's arse.

He's so small, he used to play at centre-forward for Subbuteo.

She has a face like a strangled parrot.

He was so thin that when he wore a blue suit, he looked like a refill for biros.

He was so thin that when he stood sideways and stuck his tongue out, he looked like a zip.

He was as thin as a streak of pee on a whitewashed wall.

His nose is so big that it enters a room ten seconds before he does.

She's so bowlegged she irons her bloomers over a boomerang.

She bought that dress in the sales for a ridiculous figure - her own.

She's so bowlegged that people throw her over their shoulders for good luck.

Her backside is so huge that when she bends down at Lands End, they get an eclipse at John O'Groats.

She's so bowlegged that she can walk down both sides of the street at the same time.

Did you come second in a beauty contest at Crufts?

She looks like a doughnut with a bite taken out of the bottom.

I'm not saying that you're bowlegged but you could walk down a bowling alley without disturbing the game.

I'm not saying he has a big nose but he could eat a banana in the shower without getting it wet.

He's so bowlegged, he couldn't stop a pig in an alleyway.

She looked like a DEAD HEAT in a Zeppelin race. (Big bust)

He's a face like a bulldog licking piss off a thistle..~

I've seen bigger knockers on a doll's house.

She's a face like a bag of spanners.

He's as ugly as a bucket of frogs.

He could eat a tomato through a tennis racket.

I'm not saying he has prominent ears, but from the -back he looks like a taxi with both doors open.

Who knitted your face and dropped a stitch?

She was so thin that her boobs were in single file.

He looks like a wing nut.

You have lovely blonde hair - but why do you always dye the roots black?

He looks like the FA Cup.

Why cultivate on your face what grows wild round your arse? (BEARD)

She'd the face of a Saint - Bernard.

Her face is so wrinkled, it looks like the first edition of the Dead Sea Scrolls.

He was so cross-eyed, he could watch a tennis match without moving his head.

She was so cross-eyed that when she cried, the -tears ran down her back..

Her forehead is so wrinkled, she can screw her hat on her head.

She was so thin that if she'd had another navel, she'd have been a flute.

She's so ugly that when she tries to put lipstick on, the lipstick backs down the tube.

She was so thin that when she walked near a snooker table, they chalked the top of her head.

Are those your own legs or are you breaking them in for a sparrow?

She's got a face that looks like it had rollers in it.

He's a face like a punchbag with ears.

You look like you've just been exhumed.

Why don't you wear a yellow tie to match your teeth?

Does Worzel Gummidge know you've got his head?

What would it take to get me to kiss you? Chloroform.

Is it true that when you were a baby, you were so ugly that your parents used to wrap the nappy round your face and stick the dummy up your behind?

She's had her face lifted so many times that now she's got a beard.

I've seen better legs on a snooker table.

Your face has a lived-in look. It looks as though pigs have lived in it.

Your spare tyre needs a re-tread.

Your face is like something out of a fairy tale - it's Grimm.

There's not a lot you can do about your face - but you could stay at home.

I dig your wife - is that how you got her?

I wouldn't say she was ugly but she'd be safe in a roomful of drunken sailors on shore leave.

I'll tell you a joke that'll knock your tits off. Oh - I see you've already heard it. (FLAT CHEST)

Are you two ladies sisters? And have you left Cinderella at home again?
He's so obese that when he's making love to his girlfriend, it looks like a gang bang.

She's so obese that her knicker elastic once snapped and cut down four trees.

She's so ugly that if she lived in India, she'd be sacred.

I wouldn't say he was a loud dresser, but his jacket gets complaints from the Noise Abatement Society.

She's so ugly that when she undresses for bed, Peeping Toms knock on the door and ask her to close the curtains.

Of course I remember your name. It's your face I'm trying to forget.

She has so many chins, it's as though, she's looking at you over a pile of crumpets.

She has everything that a man could desire - big biceps, a moustache and a big hairy chest.

You've got a good head on your shoulders. Whose is it?

You're face is your misfortune.

Is it true that you're a model - for gargoyles?

You've got a face like a line of wet washing.

Is it true that you were so ugly as a kid that your mother used to pull the pram?

When she walks down the street, everyone looks twice. They can't believe it the first time.

His mother died shortly after giving birth to him. She took one look at him - then shot herself.

Did you fall asleep in a greenhouse? (TALL PERSON)

Is that a beard - or are you just acting the goat?

You must have grown up when meat was cheap. (FAT PERSON)

Why don't you' rent your face out to a ratcatcher?

I've often seen people like you before - but I've usually had to buy a ticket first.

I wouldn't say she was small, but she has mudflaps on her knickers..
She once bought a mudpack to improve her looks. It worked for a couple of hours - then it dropped off.

He's so fat that when he swims in the sea, he's listed as a danger to shipping.

It's a shame for her - she has no visible means of support. (THIN LEGS)

Did your mother have any kids that lived?

I'm not saying she's big but she has a job at the airport - kick-starting Jumbo Jets.

I like your trousers - is there a circus in town?

You can't be two-faced. You wouldn't be wearing the one you are now.

Why don't you throw your hat away - and keep your head in it?

She's so huge that when she takes a bath, she has to walk naked through a carwash.

What time do you have to be back in the cemetery?

They call him Long John Silver, because he has a sunken chest.

Have you been to the beauty parlour recently? And was it shut?

Why don't you keep Britain tidy. Emigrate!

He's so small that his first job was as a hod carrier for Lego.

I wouldn't say he was short, but when he pulls up his socks he blindfolds himself.

I'd drink champagne from your shoe - but I don't think I could manage eight pints of it.

I wouldn't say he had a pot belly, but he was taller lying down than most people are standing up.

Stand by my side. I could do with something to keep the flies off me.

She's so hideous that when she had a coming-out party, they made her go back in again!
She's so fat, even her knees have double chins.

That's a nice suit - did you crumple it yourself?

Do you put your make-up on with a spraygun?

If you ever gave birth, I wouldn't want one of the puppies.

I've seen sexier eyes in a potato.

You have a neck like a swan - a black swan.

I wouldn't say she's a prominent chin, but she can prop herself up without using her elbows.

I must congratulate your tailor on his sense of humour.

She's got tits like spaniel's ears.

The seat of his trousers is so shiny that if he tore it, he'd get seven years' bad luck.

Her bra fits her better back to front.

She's got a good ear for music - it's shaped like a trombone.

Her hair looks like an explosion in a mattress factory.

Do you think that dress you're wearing will ever come back in fashion?

The airline companies put a picture of his face on the bottom of their sick bags.

He doesn't know whether he's Eddie or Edie.

I like your dress - it's marvellous what you can do with a sugar bag.

What a lovely floral design. You look like a well-kept grave.

I've never seen a face like yours since Captain Hook wiped his bottom with the wrong hand.

She says that her pot belly is just puppy fat. It's true - she looks like she swallowed a dog.

It's a shame - his mother wanted a boy.

Next to you, the Elephant Man would look normal.

Marriage lines for maximum matrimonial mayhem...

He: Did you enjoy it when we made love just then?
She: Of course I did. Didn't you hear me laughing?

She's been married so many times, her face is covered in rice marks.

He wears the trousers in his house - but his wife tells him which pair to put on.

She thinks her husband is the salt of the earth -that's why she keeps him in the cellar.

Why don't you go home and give your wife one -just like all your mates do?

His wife suffers from marital thrombosis. She married a clot.

She asked her husband to buy her a ring that matched the colour of her eyes - so he bought her a ruby.

The only way she could have had a white wedding would have been if it had snowed.

He calls his wife 'Treasure' because when people see her they say: 'Where the hell did you dig that up from?'

As she said to her husband on their honeymoon: 'You're living proof that your father was bad in bed.'

Somebody ran off with his wife and got arrested for bagsnatching.

She's been married so many times that the organist didn't play Here Comes the Bride, he played Here We Are Again.

I remember my wedding day as if it was yesterday - and you know what a bloody awful day that was!

His wife is so suspicious - even her eyes watch each other.

They wanted a quiet wedding - so her father put a silencer on the shotgun.

They went to visit her relatives last night - but the zoo gates were shut.

When they were courting, he could have eaten her. After they married, he wished that he had.

She fell for her husband hook, line and stinker.

I wouldn't say his wife was ugly, but she's the only woman I know who looks like her passport photograph.

They're sexually compatible - they both get headaches at the same time.

When, she told him she wanted an animal skin coat 11 for her birthday, he bought her a donkey-jacket.

Whenever they make love together, his wife uses him to time an egg

Marriage is like a bath - it's not so hot once you get used to it.

His wife is so ugly that when he makes love to her, he has to hire a stand-in.

She's so ugly that after the wedding, everybody kissed the groom instead.

Does he love his wife? Why he worships the ground that's coming to her.

His wife is such a lousy cook that pygmies dip their darts in her gravy. .

He remembers every wedding anniversary – he throws bricks through the windows of the church.

Her husband spent six days in the Premature Ejaculation Unit at the local infirmary. His wife said it was touch and go at one stage.

His wife doesn't pick his suits - just his pockets.

When he met his wife, it was love at first fright.

Her cooking is so bad that the mice suck Rennies . . . and the dog begs for Settlers.

They have the only dustbin on the street with ulcers.

She wanted something to improve her looks, so her husband bought her a gas mask.

They stick together through thick and thin. She's thick and he's thin.

They're a fastidious couple. She's fast and he's hideous.

She's so naive that when her husband gave her The Joy of Sex she coloured it in.

She calls her husband 'Vesuvius' - because he's always belching and dropping ash.

He took his wife to Tussaud's Chamber of Horrors and the manager said 'Keep her moving sir -we're stocktaking.'

She's only twenty-two and she's had five husbands already - one of her own and four of somebody else's.

He's a dedicated angler - in fact he only married his wife because she had worms. . .

His wife is so ugly that he wouldn't let her on their wedding photos.

His wife ran off with the man next door - and oh, he does miss him.

His wife talks through her nose- her mouth is worn out.

His wife got rid of 160 lbs of surplus fat. She divorced him.

On their honeymoon night he told his wife he was gay - then couldn't face her in bed again.

Are you married - or happy?

For thirty years, he and his wife were perfectly happy - then they met.

They've had seven happy years together - but they've been married for twenty-five.

Are you married - or have you always been round-shouldered?

When they make love doggy-fashion, he sniffs her arse and she growls.

He takes his wife with him everywhere he goes -it saves him having to kiss her goodbye.

Their house is so dirty that they have a pig in the living-room as an air-freshener.

He calls his wife 'Martini' because she's ready for it any time, any place, anywhere.

They once opened an Airwick in the house and it went back down the spout waving a white flag.

How to deal with stupid people...

DUMBO JESTS: Taking the mickey out of a thickey . . . .

She's like the Venus De Milo - nice looking, but not all there.

They crossed him with an ape - and got a mentally retarded gorilla.

If brains were gunpowder, you wouldn't have enough to blow off your cap.

Is it true you were the world's first brain transplant donor?

He's as thick as a gurkha's foreskin.

He doesn't know the meaning of the word fear -or 50,000 other words if it comes to that.

Put your hat on - there's a woodpecker about.

Why don't you have a good crap and clear your head?

Why don't you make friends with an idiot, then you'd have somebody to look up to?

They named a town after him - Leatherhead.

He's as dim as a Toc H lamp

You're as interesting as watching paint dry.

He's the only person I know who can spill Vaseline.

He suffers from varicose brains.

You have the IQ of a geranium.

You must have grown up when fish was scarce

He's as thick as a tin of paint.

She once moved from Manchester to Liverpool to be nearer her son. He lives in New York .

He's so thick he couldn't pour pee out of a boot if the instructions were written on the heel.

I was just going to do an impression of an idiot -but you've beaten me to it.

He couldn't find his bum with both hands in a fog.

He has to buy toilet rolls with instructions for use printed on them.

She's so dim she has to take off her sweater to count up to two.

He once phoned Interpol to order some flowers for his mother.

His face is full of holes because he's learning to eat - with a fork.

When you go to the hairdressers, how much a corner does he charge to cut your hair?

His father mentioned him in his will. It said: 'Hello stupid.. .'

When they wanted to know his age, they cut off the top of his head and counted the rings.

When I say you're a wit, I'm half right.

He wears his sideburns behind his ear.

If you ever needed a brain operation, the surgeon would have to charge you a search fee.

He stands outside brothels waiting for the red light to change to green so that he can go inside.

When his girlfriend said 'Wriggle it in', he thought she was talking about corrugated iron.

If he were a turkey, he would be looking forward to Christmas.

He once asked a Lesbian which part of Lesbia she came from.

He once spent three hours trying to slam shut a revolving door.

He thought he'd save himself the trouble of growing a beard by buying three tins of Whiskas from the pet shop.

He was putting some toilet water on his face -and the seat fell on his head.

He once saw a peach and thought it was a velvet apple.

He once went into British Home Stores to try and buy a bungalow.,

He's as useless as a one-legged man at an arse-kicking contest.

Why don't you shove a stick of dynamite up your bum and blow your brains out?

He had his house moved back six feet to take up the slack in his clothesline.

He stayed up all night studying for a urine test.

Why don't you use your brain as a door-stop?

When a man at a dance asked her if he could see her home, she showed him a picture of her council-house.

He scores nil on the brainometer.

He went to night school because he thought he was going to learn how to read in the dark.

I wish I had an IQ low enough to enjoy your company.

He mended twenty-six windows in his house then found out it was a crack in his glasses.

He sold his water skis because he couldn't find a lake on a hill.

She once heard that ninety per cent of all road accidents happen within a five-mile radius of the home - so she moved house.

He's full of brotherly love - he hates to see anyone beating a donkey.

Education's a wonderful thing - you should get one sometime.

He once went into a. pub and ordered soup in a basket.

He once complained to a zookeeper that the snakes kept pulling their tongues out at him.

She once applied for a job knitting toupees for bald tyres.

She says she's an intellectual because all her tattoos are spelt correctly.

He once saw a sign saying 'Wet Paint', so he peed on it.

There are more brains in a rocking-horse.

He's' got fresh air keeping his ears apart.

She's got a bust of 38 - and an IQ to match.

He's so stupid that if he got a gas leak, he'd put a bucket under it.

You can confuse her by just saying 'Good Morning' to' her.

He puts real mice in Bubble and Squeak.

He was such a slow developer that his mother had to breast-feed him through the school railings.

She's so naive that she thinks her husband is a clever bloke because he's always helping the police with their inquiries..

Burglars broke into his library last night ~ and stole both his colouring books.

He once locked his keys in the car and used a coathanger to get his family out.

He\She's so stupid, he\she thinks that….

- backgammon is a pig's bum.

- highballs are something on a giraffe. - Fanny Hill is a beauty spot off the M1.

- an itchy fanny is a Japanese motor-bike.

- Sherlock Holmes is a block of flats.

- Hitler's first name was 'Heil'.

- Wanking is a province of China .

- Slim Panatella's a Country and Western singer.

- Alberto Balsam is a member of the Mafia.

- Pubic Hair was Brer Rabbit's brother.

- Walls of Jericho was the world's first ice-cream manufacturers.

- Moby Dick's a social disease.

- a Zulu's a lavatory at Whipsnade.

- Bristol Cream is what women rub on sore nipples.

- the Dog Star is Lassie.

-thinks a nut case is a cricketer's box.

- a good screw is a friendly prison warder.

- cubicles are square testicles.

- an innuendo is an Italian suppository.

- virgin wool is a sheep that's faster than a Welsh shepherd.

- ping pong balls is a medical complaint.

How to lash a loudmouth.

Next time you open your mouth, we'll all jump in.

She never wears lipstick - because she can never keep her mouth still long enough to put it on.

You remind me of a river - wide at the mouth.

Would you mind standing up - I'd like to see if the rest of you is as big as your mouth.

The difference between you and a motorway is that you can turn off a motorway.

Why don't you hold your breath for a minute and make me happy? On second thoughts, hold your breath for twenty minutes and make everybody happy.

When God gave you teeth, he spoiled a bloody good arse.

She's got a mouth so big that she can hold three billiard balls in it without getting a cannon.

Why don't you do what your head does and come to the point?

I used to think that was a wart on your chin -until I found out it was a grease nipple.

There's a drop of beer at the corner of your mouth - just below your ear.

If his wallet were as big as his mouth, he'd be a very rich man.

You think you're a comedian. You should turn pro - just like your mother did.

She has a tongue like a length of tripe.

She's the kind of woman you phone up and hope you get the engaged signal.

They tried to take an X-ray of her jaw but all they got was a blur.

I'm not saying he has a big mouth, but when he was in hospital, they used to take his temperature with a barometer.

When she goes abroad for her holidays, she comes back with a sunburned tongue.

He puts his mouth into gear before he engages his brain.

I'm not saying she has a big mouth, but she keeps her false teeth in a bucket.

She can't swim because-she can't keep her mouth shut for long enough.

You'd make deafness a pleasure.

The last time I saw a mouth like yours, Tarzan was feeding it bananas - sideways.

The last time I saw a mouth like yours, it had a hook in it.

I've got a good gag for you - to fit right over your mouth.

Why don't you put a landing light on your nose and use your tongue as a runway?

If his mouth was any bigger, he'd have no face left to wash.

A lie never passes his lips - he always talks through his arse.

He throws peanuts in the air and catches them in his mouth - two bags at a time.

He's just like a little bird - all shit and twitter.

Why don't you sit down and give your brains a rest?

As I slide down the bannister of life, I shall always remember you as a splinter in the bum.

He can whisper over three fields - Huddersfield , Mansfield and Sheffield .

His mouth is so big that he can sing a duet by himself.

They call him the Atlantic Ocean - because that never dries up either

You should be on the Parole Board - you never let anybody finish a sentence.

She could start an argument in an empty house.

She talks so much that her fillings have metal fatigue.

The world's biggest sucker -

- jacknifed his Mini.

- complained to the council that he had a big pool of water in his back yard - and they sent him three ducks.

- bought his wife a vibrator and it went limp.

- fell in a barrel of tits and came out sucking his thumb.

- came third in a duel.

- bought a suit with two pairs of trousers, then burned a hole in the jacket.

- bought some artificial flowers for his wife - and they died.

- found out that health food makes him ill.

- caught pimples off Germolene.

- bought a packet of Polos and all the holes were on the outside..

- dropped dead after drinking a can of Long Life.

- waited for his ship to come in and it turned out to be the Titanic.

- heard opportunity knocking and thought it was his knees. .

- went to his wife's cremation and got a cinder in -his eye. .

- is so unlucky that if he was one of triplets born to Dolly Parton, he'd be the one on the bottle.

- had a kidney transplant from a bed wetter.

- caught herpes off a blow-up doll.

- once bought a duck and it sank.

- peeled himself a banana - and found it was empty .

GONE - BUT FORG0TTEN . . .

The old country folk were never short of an apt word or two to
describe those they felt deserving of their scorn.
Here then, from the turn of the century, are some choice colourful
dialect epithets from various parts of the British Isles which are
sadly no longer part of the vocal currency. However, please feel free
to resurrect them.

Flopsydoll.
Slattern (SOUTH NOTTS)

Zawk.
Fool. (SOUTH DEVON)

Blether-breeks.
Braggart. (NORTHUMBERLAND)

Clap-tongue.
Gossip. (SOUTH CHESHIRE)

Spew-faced.
White-faced. (NORTH YORKS)

Jerry-me-diddler!
Ignorant good-for-nothing. (GLOUCS)

As soft as me pocket.
Foolish. (WORCS)

All gob and guts.
A talkative greedy person. (NORTHUMBERLAND)

Trolly-bags!
Corpulent, ungainly person. (LAKE DISTRICT)

Bum-sucker!
A toady. (WEST SOMERSET)

Shit-pot.
A sneak. (YORKSHIRE)

Muckworm.
Sordid or avaricious person. (NORTHANTS)

Kick-hammer.
Stammerer. (SOMERSET)

Snotter-gob.
Contemptible person. (LANCASHIRE)

He hasn't sense to bait a mouse-trap.
Fool. (NORTH LINCS)

Gob-a-Tosh.
Person with prominent teeth. (WEST YORKS)

Taw-Pie.
Fool. (ORKNEYS) ,

Narrow-arsed.
Mean. (CUMBERLAND)

Wench-faced.
Without any whiskers. (LINCS)

Buzgut!
Glutton. (CORNWALL)

Ride-the- Moon.
Wild dissipated fellow. (WEST YORKS)

Snotgobbler.
Most unpleasant person (LANCASHIRE)

Rattle-bag.
Noisy person. (SCOTLAND)

Greet Buzzom!
Simpleton. (NORTHUMBERLAND)

Blaitie Bum.
Idle person. (FIFESHIRE)

Sour-Zab.
Ill-tempered person. (DEVON)

As soft as a boiled turnip.
Easily given to tears. (EAST YORKS)

Cold Water Man.
Abstainer. (SCOTLAND)

Gew-mouthed.
Idiot-faced. (FLAMBOROUGH)

Flyte-poke.
Double-chin. (SCOTLAND)

Pappy.
Puffed up with pride. (SCOTLAND)

Washamouth!
Foul-mouth (SOMERSET)

Chubble-headed.
Foolish. (DEVON)

Sour-Sop.
Ill-natured person. (ISLE OF WIGHT)

Siss.
Fat Woman. (DEVON)

Fat Dabs.
Large overweight awkward person. (N.E. YORKS)

Moozles.
Slow, stupid, slovenly person (LINCS)

You know you're in a rough area when...

- the local pub has plasma on draught behind the bar.

- the local public convenience has soap on the end of a chain.

- the coppers go round in pairs *inside* the police station. .

- the muggers are frightened to go out at night.

- the vicar's an atheist.

- the infants school kids are selling tickets for the headmaster's ball and it isn't a dance, it's a raffle.

- they have to have a bloke riding shotgun on the milk-float.

- you put out your hand to signal a right turn in your car and somebody nicks your watch.

- you're frightened of slamming a window down in case you trap someone's fingers.

- people borrow a cup of sugar off the next-door-neighbour until the corner shop shuts.

- the jewellers' shops have only knives and forks in the window

- the kids make the *teachers* stay behind after school!

Dave's other books include The Book of Famous Oddballs (bizarre, true facts about famous folk); Horrors! (true gruesome and macabre tales) and How to Be a Crafty Cruiser (money and time-saving tips and tricks for cruise holidays. All available from most major ebook publishers and on Amazon.

Printed in Great Britain
by Amazon